Wine
Pairing Party

Wine
Pairing Party

16 wine profiles
80 perfect food pairings

BY LIZ RUBIN

CHRONICLE BOOKS
SAN FRANCISCO

THE WINES

Sparkling

Champagne and Crémant

Prosecco

Pet-Nat

White

Sauvignon Blanc

Chardonnay

Riesling (Sweet)

Rosé

Provençal Rosé

Pinot Noir and Gamay Rosé

Italian Rosé

Light Reds

Pinot Noir

Gamay

Frappato

Dark Reds

Zinfandel

Bordeaux

Syrah

Dessert Wines

Introduction

Through our unique cultural, spiritual, and regional experiences, we naturally become accustomed to pairing certain food and drink together. Our entire sense of taste is constructed in this way. A parent or another family member, crafting our school lunches, becomes the first arbiter of flavor creation and good taste in our lives. These early pairings become implicit in how we understand food. When I was little, Oscar Mayer Lunchables were extremely popular. In a basic way, these circles of meat and squares of cheese were the first charcuterie boards children of the '90s were exposed to. I was all about it!

When we are younger we strive to blend in with the immediate world around us, and food is one key element to demonstrate whether we are following the status quo or deviating from established norms. As we grow up we become exposed to other people's and cultures' ideas of food pairings, and that expands our minds and palates exponentially. We experiment and we tinker with what tastes delicious to us, and this helps us understand the elements needed for a balanced taste.

Adding wine to a pairing is understandably daunting. It can bring with it a seriousness that can take us away from whimsical experimenting and fun. Wine should be understood as simply more flavor to play with. Each type of wine introduces new aromas, textures, and elements of bitterness, tartness, piquancy, and earthiness that only extend the possibilities of where the pairing can go.

How to Use This Book

Having worked in the retail wine industry for the past ten years, I have learned that most people have a hard time describing what they like and asking for it. The "if-you-don't-know-you-shouldn't-bother-to-ask" idea prevents people from asking questions to better their understanding. Ironically, at the same time, I have noticed consumers becoming more flavor fluent with food. They have become more adept at using an expanded pantry full of different flavors, while social media has made recipes easy to be disseminated and edited. I want wine to be thought of in the same way, so one of the aims of this book is to break down wines into distinct flavors and help you understand them as ingredients that support the dishes you create.

This is not a book about wine. This is a book about pairing wine *with* food. It's divided into five sections: sparkling, whites, rosés, light reds, and dark reds. Each of the five sections is then broken up into three types of wine. Each type of wine carries particular flavor notes, textural profiles, and distinct body characteristics. The wine types are supported with four pairings, a recipe, and a "fun fact." The purpose here is to give you the tools to create perfect pairings.

The Key Is Always Balance ...

Let's take the example of making a homemade stew (like Mom's Bolognese) you've made many times before. The first step is creating a base of flavor: You've added a mirepoix of aromatic vegetables, an herb bundle, salt, and pepper and you are letting everything caramelize. Next you add the meat and let the fat render and combine with the caramelized vegetables. Liquid—either stock or canned tomatoes and cooking wine—is added next to create a rich sauce. After simmering for an hour or two or four, depending on the recipe, you taste. When you do, you are taking stock of the flavors you have versus the flavors you are lacking. Do you need to add salt, pepper, a squeeze of lemon? It's easy to judge what you need when you are familiar with the recipe, but in the end, you are aiming to create a dish with balanced flavors. Pairing wine and food can also be understood in this same way. Each element in the pairing combines to create balance—when one lacks in acid, salinity, pepper, or sweetness, another element contributes. Wine should be simply thought of as one element in the pairing that is contributing flavor.

Basic Glossary of Wine Vocabulary

ACIDITY: Acidity is the brightness that is associated with malic acid or acid found in fruit juice.

BODY: Body is the impression of weight the wine leaves on your palate. Fuller-bodied wines linger longer, as they tend to coat the inside of your mouth. Both whites and reds can be described as having a lighter or fuller body.

EARTH: Earthy wines have flavors that resemble the forest floor, rich soil, and roots.

FRUIT: Fruity wines have flavors reminiscent of fresh fruit. Common fruit expressions are tropical fruits, red fruits like raspberry and cranberry, blue fruits like blueberry, and black fruits like blackberry.

MINERALITY: Wines grown in mineral-rich soil display a flavor profile that is associated with rocks and metals.

SALINITY: Salinity is the saltiness that is usually associated with the maritime influence of certain vineyards.

SPICE: Spice-driven wines possess flavors of pantry spices—clove, cinnamon, anise, and pepper are common.

TERROIR: In its basic definition, terroir is the sense-based characteristics that define a place where the wine was cultivated. Taking the grape type out of the equation, soil type and geology, climate, and geography are the key elements of the terroir of a wine, as these factors determine how one wine differs from another wine.

How to Taste Wine

Wine tasting can really be divided into four aspects: sight, smell, taste, and understanding.

SIGHT: You can learn a tremendous amount about wine before you taste it. Body can be judged by the viscosity or "legs" that are present on the sides of a glass. The more viscous or syrupy the wine, the weightier it will be on your palate. The color in the glass can give clues to the amount of oak or simply the aging time. A tawny-colored wine can oftentimes mean it has spent more time aging in an oak barrel, whereas a bright ruby tone could signal youth and/or steel aging.

SMELL: Smelling a wine can give you a more complete picture of the story of a wine. Swirling the wine opens it up to oxygen in the air, releasing more olfactory nuance. Do you smell fruit or floral tones? These are elements of *primary aromas* that can be associated with the grape varietal(s). *Secondary aromas* are oftentimes funky, cheesy, or astringent and are derived from the process of winemaking. Finally, aromas of spices like vanilla or tobacco are called *tertiary aromas* and can be associated with fermentation or aging vessels imparting influence on the wine.

TASTE: Your tongue is highly effective in detecting sour- ness, salinity, sweetness, and bitterness, which are flavor elements harder to differentiate by smell. Textural differ- ences can come from higher alcohol, residual sugar, or tannin, and through tasting, we can best understand the root causes of textural change.

UNDERSTANDING: The intellectual aspect of tasting is just as important as the other facets. This is the part where we step back and piece all the information together and try to gather a story to form meaning. We need this perspective to understand the parts of the whole.

What Makes a Good Pairing

Nowadays, many people have probably attended a pairing class of sorts, or at least have been interested in one. It's that "next-level" idea that can experientially change a meal into a great moment. Pairing wine with food can be an intimidating process, but the great thing is you don't have to know a lot about wine to understand when a pairing is successful. The main questions to keep in mind are the following: Can I still taste each constituent part of the pairing when I taste them together? Does one overpower the other? Is it delicious?

It may be helpful to think of every pairing in terms of a first date. In our experience, the best dates are the ones where there is rapport. Both people are sharing their thoughts and experiences; maybe there's banter, maybe laughter ensues. Similarly, a wine can offer a lot to enhance the flavors of a food or dish and vice versa. Unsuccessful pairings, aside from not tasting good, occur when one element of the pairing overshadows the other. If we go back to the dating analogy, perhaps one person is slightly more extroverted than the other and therefore has the more dominant personality. Because of this, it seems as if the quieter person is not even present at the table. In a pairing, this less-dominant element could still taste delicious, but remember: The pairing succeeds only when both parts are represented. Ultimately, success means a lovely symbiosis of flavor. Like the phrase "opposites attract," some of the best pairings occur with two opposite yet complementary elements—salty with sweet is just one example. Successful pairings can also change minds. Blue cheese tends to be one of the more contentious flavors for people, but acceptance and even enjoyment often follow a pairing with fruit compote and tawny port.

Here is a simple scale that you can use to grade each pairing:

+3

A +3 pairing experience is extremely rare and memorable. It means that the elements of the pairing are better together than separate. This is an alchemical moment when new flavors emerge that were unexpected. These are the pairings that can move you to tears, like hearing beautiful music or seeing a fine piece of art.

+2

This is a pairing that ticks all the boxes! Each element of the pairing can be tasted in the presence of the others and everything tastes great together.

+1

This is the instance where one or some elements of the pairing are elevated over others. The result still tastes good, but the pairing is disjointed and therefore not truly successful.

0

Zero means nothing lost and nothing gained. The pairing had no synergy, the date no rapport.

-1

This is the mirror to the +1 pairing. Here, one or some elements of the pairing are elevated over others, but in this instance the pairing tastes lousy. It is unbalanced and not delicious.

-2

This pairing is balanced in that all elements are present, yet the pairing is unsuccessful because it does not taste appealing.

-3

A -3 pairing is an utter failure and, quite frankly, disgusting.

The Setup: Glassware and Decanting

It is not necessary to use different-shaped glasses in order
to enhance the tasting experience for each varietal or
style of wine. The main objective for determining which
glass to use should center around aeration: when wine is
exposed to oxygen. For a versatile choice, a simple white
wine glass shape allows for ideal aeration for most wines,
even sparkling. A flute, the glass that is most often used
for Champagne and other sparkling wine, is the least
functionally shaped glass for tasting wine. It is too small
and too tapered to fully grasp the nuances of a wine like
Champagne, which can be extremely complex in flavor,
texture, and body. Don't be afraid to experiment with
different glass shapes and different wines to see how your
experience changes, but know that you do not need to
spend money on Burgundy and Bordeaux glasses in order
to drastically improve your experience.

Decanting can be a useful way to open up a stubborn
wine that is not very expressive, which can be caused
by reductive winemaking. Traditionally, wines are made
more oxidatively, which means they are exposed to
air during the process of fermentation. By creating an
anaerobic (i.e., limited exposure to air) environment, a

winemaker may be trying to preserve its primary taste characteristics, like fruit presence. We see this mostly with wines that are meant to age—bigger reds like Bordeaux or Syrah, where the true flavors cannot happen for years. The concept of a wine "needing time" may reflect this reductive state, which acts like a chrysalis protecting the wine until the wine can be fully realized.

Reductive wines tend to have more sulfuric notes like cabbage or rubber and are particularly unpleasant smelling. You may think a wine has gone bad or is corked, but in actuality it is as if it is merely asleep. By decanting the wine, the anaerobic state is broken by a flood of oxygen, and the reductive nature of the wine begins to "blow off." This would eventually occur in the glass with heavy swirling and exposure to air, but the decanter accelerates the process.

The downside to decanting is that it can, in effect, age a wine too quickly. The primary aromas are the first to evaporate, and you begin to notice secondary and tertiary aroma characteristics. I avoid decanting because I enjoy experiencing the natural progression of how a wine changes over time, but I understand the reasons why some may want to quicken this process. Also, there's no need to buy a fancy decanter—the bottle the wine comes from can act as a decanter of sorts; just leave it open for a length of time and come back to it later.

Champagne and Crémant

Fresh and Fatty Cheese

**Triple-cream cheeses
(e.g., Brillat-Savarin or Saint André)**
Chèvre (local fresh goat cheese)
Alpine styles (e.g., Comté or Gruyère)

Both the acid and effervescence of Champagne and crémant work very well with the lactic fat of cheese. When in doubt, regional pairings are fun and usually successful; try Comté and Crémant du Jura Blanc or Champagne and Chaource.

Cured Meats

Prosciutto
Speck
Soppressata

Cured pork fat is a magical pairing with Champagne and crémant rosé. The bright red fruit notes complement the gamey notes in the meat, and the bubbles cut through the fat. Be mindful of the spice profile in the meat, as sometimes too much heat or pepper can overpower the wine. Soppressata is a more versatile salami; Finocchiona or Calabrese might be more limiting.

For me, Champagne is that perfect bookend. Its bright acid and delicacy make it a wonderful aperitif to ready the palate for what's to come, and its freshness and minerality serve to restore your palate after a rich meal. The best Champagne pairings keep in check the balance of acid, as too much of it can be astringent. If you like it lean and more delicate, try a non-vintage Chardonnay Champagne, known as a Blanc de Blancs. For a richer and more powerful note, try one with more Pinot Noir in the blend. Champagne with a higher percentage of Pinot Meunier (a grape varietal) can evoke fruit notes, which gives it another dimension of pairing potential.

Flavors to Look For

- White flowers—Crémant d'Alsace
- Honey—Crémant du Jura
- Citrus pith and flesh—Champagne
- Stone fruit—Crémant d'Alsace
- Red fruit—Champagne and crémant rosé

Flavors to Avoid

- Bitterness
- Astringent acidity
- Saccharin

fun fact

Rosé Champagne is sometimes produced using the *saignée* method (literally translated as "bleeding"), which is what the grape skins are doing during this short maceration. For this process, juice and must (crushed fruit containing stems, seeds, and skins) are left to ferment for a short time, giving the wine more structure and color. This style of wine acts more like a sparkling light red and therefore can be paired with more robust flavors—try it with meat-centric dishes like roast chicken or prime rib.

Pairing 3
Fried Chicken

Champagne and fried food is a no-fail pairing. There's also something about the low-brow/high-brow combination that makes it extra satisfying.

Pairing 4
Sushi

Sushi and sparkling wine is a very delicate and nuanced pairing. Whether it's the floral notes of Crémant d'Alsace, the orchard fruit notes of Crémant de Loire, or the more umami-driven profile of a Crémant du Jura, crémant complements and enhances the flavors of raw fish and soy sauce.

Champagne and Triple-Cream Cheese Pairing for New Year's Eve

This may seem like a decadent pairing (and that's because it is), but the combination of the Champagne and butter fat from the cheese will marry extremely well, leaving your palate cleansed. By removing the top rind of the Brillat-Savarin, you are creating an edible bowl of cheese to dip crusty bread into.

SERVES 6

1½ lb [680 g] round of Brillat-Savarin or other French triple-cream cheese, top rind removed

6 oz [170 g] dried fruit of your choice (dried cherries and sultanas work well)

1 baguette, sliced into rounds (or 20 to 30 crackers)

1 bottle NV (non-vintage) Blanc de Blancs Champagne

Arrange the cheese, dried fruit, and baguette on a platter and serve with glasses of Champagne.

In contrast to Champagne, a crémant is a French sparkling wine that can be made with any varietal that happens to grow in the region where the wine is made. They can range from Crémant D'Alsace (made from aromatic varietals like Pinot Blanc or Riesling) to a Crémant de Loire (made with peppery Cabernet Franc or pear-forward Chenin Blanc) to the sherry-like nuttiness of a Crémant du Jura. The versatility in both varietal and geography make crémant suitable for a larger range of pairings—try experimenting with regional dishes from the wine's area to understand its awesome adaptability.

Prosecco

Italian Prosecco is one of my favorite wines to pair with food. Like all wine, there are good and bad representations, and I think Prosecco's reputation has suffered from the influx of mass-produced versions. Most industrially made Prosecco is created by carbonating premade juice and tends to be sweeter and less interesting than the artisanally made varieties. Like Champagne, Prosecco is produced in high-altitude areas where cooler climates preserve natural acidity and aroma. The grape of Prosecco is Glera, which is of Slovenian origin but has been growing in the Veneto region of Northern Italy for hundreds of years. Italian sparkling wine can either be labeled as *frizzante*, or lightly sparkling, or *spumante*, which is full sparkling. Traditional Prosecco is often made "extra dry," which is actually less dry than "brut" and still maintains a fruity sweetness. This hint of residual sugar that often comes just from adding more fresh grape juice or must makes it a wonderful pairing agent for salty or cured foods like charcuterie, anchovies, and even briny oysters.

fun fact

Prosecco is made using the Charmat method, where secondary fermentation happens in a sealed, pressurized tank to keep in the CO_2. This highly scientific process is great for lengthening the fermentation, actually slowing it down with colder temperatures. This "low and slow" idea allows Prosecco producers to retain aromatics and acidity in the wine, while also creating a very crisp and lean texture that a barrel can sometimes round out.

Pet-Nat

Petillant Naturel, or Pet-Nat, has become all the rage in recent years. Because this type of wine is produced before fermentation is over (a process known as *Methode Ancestrale*), it tends to retain more sweetness from the grapes themselves. Most often left unfiltered, Pet-Nats have a fuller texture and mouthfeel that make them more robust and great to pair with a myriad of foods. Unlike Champagne or Prosecco, you can find Pet-Nat in all regions of the world, using any and all varietals. I prefer ones made with red grapes, as they tend to bring a greater balance of savory and sweet, which make them insanely delicious as a before-dinner aperitif with many types of appetizers. Recently, Pet-Nat has become a symbol of the natural wine movement and a style that many young winemakers the world over are employing.

fun fact

Methode Ancestrale is
the oldest style of producing
sparkling wine. It preceded the
Champagne method by
more than a century!

Sauvignon Blanc

There are many flavor profiles that comprise Sauvignon Blanc, ranging from more saline notes to an herbal, citrus prominence to a fruit-forward flavor. Sauvignon Blanc can be categorized as a light-bodied white wine that leaves less of an impression of weight on one's palate, and therefore less of a lingering layer of flavor after consuming. For the most part, Sauvignon Blanc can be described as crisp, dry, and minerally. These wines tend to be more easily paired with food, and when paired smartly, Sauvignon Blanc can cleanse and refresh the palate to ready it for more complex food flavors. This section touches on Sauvignon Blanc grown in different regions of the world, since soil types play a large role in changing the styles of these wines.

factors can have a great impact on the flavors that end up in your glass. This section will explore how best to pair food with the many faces of one of the most prolifically grown grapes: Chardonnay.

Caramelized Onion Jam

This spreadable, savory jam is a game changer: Try spreading it on a sandwich (using leftover roast chicken, perhaps?) for an umami-forward lunch.

MAKES 1 CUP [300 G]

¼ cup [55 g] butter
2 yellow onions, thinly sliced
¼ cup [60 ml] white wine

In a medium saucepan over medium heat, melt the butter. Add the onions and cook, stirring occasionally, until brown and softened, 10 to 15 minutes.

Turn down the heat to medium-low, slowly pour in the wine, and cook until the onion jam reduces to a soft and spreadable consistency, 20 to 30 minutes. Set aside to cool. The jam can be refrigerated in an airtight container for up to 5 days.

Roast Chicken

Chardonnay grown in Mâcon, which is in southern Burgundy, tends to be fuller bodied because of the region's higher composition of clay soil. Mixed with limestone, this terroir creates a balance of richness and linearity. This Chardonnay evokes flavors of cultured cream, honey, orchard fruit, and thyme. It is the perfect style of Chardonnay to go alongside roast chicken prepared with butter, herbs, and roasted root vegetables.

Indian Curry

Chardonnay grown in warmer regions like California or South America displays more of a tropical flavor profile. I love it with dishes that are assertive in spice, like spicy and creamy coconut curries. The Southeast Asian spices are perfectly married with Chardonnay's voluptuous texture and aromatic nature, and the tropical notes of mango, papaya, and lychee tend to have a cooling effect that is quite satisfying.

fun fact

BARREL FERMENTATION

Barrel fermentation is another way to add texture and body to a wine. The newer the oak, the more profound this effect can be. For the purposes of pairing, I like to stay away from wines that are fermented with a high percentage of new oak, as the flavors of the barrel are often in conflict with the flavors of the food.

Riesling (Sweet)

Pairing 1
Washed-Rind Cheeses

As a cheesemonger, I have come to trust the adage "stinky loves sweet," which means stinky and pungent cheese pairs wonderfully with sweet wine. I particularly love to use Époisses, a Burgundian cheese that is washed with brandy and allowed to develop an extremely pungent flavor and aroma that is caused by bacterial interaction. Late harvest Riesling pairs deliciously with cheeses like these because the concentration of sugars in the wine creates a syrupy texture, which envelops the funky cheese and tempers its pungent stink.

Pairing 2
Salami

An off-dry wine like a Kabinett Riesling is great with salty meats like salami because its sweetness is balanced with high acid, crunchy minerality, and salinity. It brings out the earthy funk of the fermented meat, and the sweetness pairs well with the botanicals that were used to cure the salami. I like this Riesling with pork salami, but if you can get game meats like boar and venison, all the better.

Flavors to Look Out For

- Citrus blossoms
- Herbs
- Honey
- Salt
- Acidity

Flavors to Avoid

- Cloying sweetness
- Bitterness
- Butterscotch (usually an indicator that a wine has oxidized)

I love Riesling, and I *really* love sweet Riesling. For there to be residual sugar in a wine, fermentation had to have ended before all the sugars were eaten by the yeast. This means that not only are these wines sweeter, they're also lower in alcohol, as alcohol is the byproduct of the marriage between yeast and sugar. A little residual sugar doesn't have to mean a saccharin wine, though, and a good Riesling should have an adequate amount of acidity and minerality to balance out the sugar, thanks to a terroir rich in minerals and low in altitude. Sweet Riesling, like other sweet wines, is not always best paired with sweet foods—it can even make the pairing pointedly imbalanced. A rule of thumb is extreme flavors: Sweet wines with high acid are wonderful with dishes that are heavily spiced, packed with heat, and somewhat funky.

Pavlova

4 egg whites
1¼ cups [250 g] granulated sugar
2 tsp cornstarch
1 tsp vanilla extract
1 tsp fresh lemon juice
2 cup [480 ml] heavy cream
Fresh seasonal fruit, for garnish

Preheat the oven to 300°F [150°C]. Draw a 9 in [23 cm] circle on a piece of parchment paper and line a baking sheet with the paper (the clean side of the paper facing up). In a large bowl, beat the egg whites until stiff but not dry. Gradually add in the sugar, about 1 Tbsp at a time, beating well after each addition, until thick and glossy. Gently fold in the cornstarch, vanilla, and lemon juice. Spoon the mixture inside the circle drawn on the parchment paper. Working from the center, spread the mixture toward the outside edge of the circle. Place the sheet in the oven and bake for 1 hour, then cool on a wire rack. Meanwhile, in a small bowl, beat the cream until stiff peaks form; set aside. Remove the meringue from the parchment paper and place it on a flat serving plate. Top the meringue with the whipped cream and seasonal fruit and serve.

Thai Food

Papaya salad
Larb

The level of sweetness and acid of German Spätlese Rieslings is fantastic with spicy foods. I love a Spätlese with Thai dishes like papaya salad or larb that are packed with fish sauce, lemongrass, chile, and herbs. The umami, sweet, and sour notes of these dishes bring out flavors that already exist in the wine, and the heat is the perfect complement to the wine's acid and viscosity.

Pavlova

Auslese has a floral sweetness that is very delicate and never too cloying. I love Auslese with pavlova, a meringue-based dessert that is studded with fresh fruit and enriched with citrus curd and whipped cream. The wine brings out the acid and floral notes of the fresh fruit, and the curd tempers the sweetness of the wine and meringue. It's a delicate dessert and a wonderful pairing.

fun fact

BOTRYTIS

Botrytis, otherwise known as noble rot, is a fungus that attacks wine grapes and creates more concentrated sugars that produce sweet wines. It usually does this by killing the yeast that keeps fermentation going. Sweet Rieslings and dessert wines like Sauternes and Tokaji are the most famous wines that incorporate botrytised grapes in their processes.

Provençal Rosé

Fresh Cheese

Chèvre
Fresh sheep's milk
Ricotta

Fresh cheese and Provençal rosé can be a perfect pairing, as the herbal and citrus notes in the wine elegantly evoke the animal nuance in the cheese. Fresh sheep's milk and cow's milk cheeses are often milder than goat cheese, so make sure you are choosing the right rosé for the pairing.

Prosciutto and Country Ham

The delicate cure on prosciutto and country ham is a lovely salty-and-sweet accompaniment to Provençal rosé.

Flavors to Look For

- Herbs
- Black pepper
- White pepper
- Blood
- Citrus
- Salt

Flavors to Avoid

- Metallic notes
- Cooked fruit

Provençal rosé should not be thought of as anything less than a serious wine. This style is characterized by a more mineral-driven flavor profile, so it often tastes like the soil composition in which the grape vines were grown. Provence, where this wine is produced, is the oldest wine region in France and the geology is very diverse: To the west is limestone, to the east is granite and volcanic rock, while both gain influence from the Mediterranean Sea. All of this adds to the flavor profile of this wine. Sea-loving vegetation, as well as the salt water itself, give the wine a savory quality that makes it easier to pair with food. Bandol and Cassis are probably the two most famous wine-producing areas in Provence. In both of these regions, red and white wine grapes are fermented to make the blends for the rosé. Depending on the blend, the color of Provençal rosé can be pale salmon to very dark hued. Maceration, or the amount of time the juice spent gaining color from the skin, can make a rosé more vinous (meaning it has a powerful and assertive flavor more often associated with red wine) and therefore give it the chops to pair with bolder flavors. Don't be afraid to age it, as the mineral backbone and acidity can withstand the test of time.

Frozé!

Who doesn't love a boozy blended drink now and again? This recipe can easily be scaled up for a party (or to freeze, so you can have Frozé at the ready).

SERVES 4

Ice
1½ cups [360 ml] rosé (approximately half of a 750 ml [25 oz] bottle)
¼ cup [60 ml] simple syrup

Fill a blender halfway with ice and add the rosé and simple syrup. Blend until smooth and serve immediately. Store any extra in an airtight container in the freezer and reblend with an extra dash of rosé to reconstitute.

Pairing 3
Roast Chicken

Bandol rosé and roast chicken make for a sublime pairing. Roast the chicken with herbs, sea salt, and butter to bring out the best notes in the rosé.

Pairing 4
Milk-Fed Lamb

Most of the new rosés come out in the spring, and so does the season's milk-fed lamb. This protein is milder than the grass-fed version and is perfect with the mineral-driven rosé.

fun fact

GARIGUE

Garigue is the name given to the Mediterranean vegetation that dots the landscape of southwestern France. This vegetation is primarily herbs—thyme, lavender, rosemary, and tarragon. Garigue is a primary tasting note of wine produced in this region and serves to augment the wines' profiles.

Pinot Noir and Gamay Rosé

Pairing 1

Fresh Goat Cheese

The salty, acidic cheese is wonderful with the fruitier rosé, creating a berry cheesecake–flavored combination.

Pairing 2

Labneh with Sumac and Fresh Herbs

Sumac is a spice that is inherently citrusy. I love to sprinkle liberal amounts on labneh (strained sheep's milk yogurt). The sumac and the acidic yet lactic yogurt pair perfectly with a crisp rosé. Serve with naan, pita, or lavash and cucumber and tomato slices for a complete lunchtime spread.

Flavors to Look For

- Sour cherry
- Pomegranate
- Cranberry
- Orchard blossom

Flavors to Avoid

- Candied fruit

When you are looking for a rosé that is dry yet less minerally, try a rosé made with Pinot Noir and Gamay. You can find them from domestic producers in California and Oregon, but they are also prevalent all over the world; some of my favorites are from Germany and the Loire Valley in France. Most Pinot Noir and Gamay rosés are made in the style known as *direct press*, which means the grapes are pressed with the intention of making rosé and are created with light maceration. The resulting wine is often delicate and fruity with a paler hue. Because these grapes are grown all over the world, the wines differ based on terroir. If you are looking for a fruitier rosé, choosing one of the Californian- or Oregon-made wines is a good idea.

Spiced Pita Chips

This recipe is super versatile, so feel free to try different spices and find the combination you like best. In place of za'atar, try Aleppo pepper, garlic powder, paprika, or a mixture of each.

SERVES 2

2 whole pitas
¼ cup [60 ml] extra-virgin olive oil
1 Tbsp za'atar
1 Tbsp sesame seeds

Preheat the oven to 350°F [180°C]. Line a baking sheet with aluminum foil.

Cut each pita into eight wedges (you will have sixteen wedges total). Spread the pita wedges on the prepared baking sheet and brush with the olive oil. In a small bowl, combine the za'atar and sesame seeds. Sprinkle the spice mixture over the pita wedges. Bake in the oven for 10 minutes, or until crisp and lightly browned. Let the pita chips sit at room temperature until cool and store in a sealed bag for up to 1 week.

Lamb Merguez Sausage

If your merguez isn't made with herbs, I would accompany this dish with a sauce made of mint. It's wonderful with the bright and juicy rosé.

Middle Eastern Food

Baba ghanoush

Fattoush

Olives and fresh cheese

Hummus

Falafel

All the flavors of Middle Eastern food are wonderful with fruity rosé of Pinot Noir and Gamay. Spices like za'atar, sumac, and cumin and condiments like pomegranate molasses and yogurt are simply perfect paired with the high acid and red fruit of these wines.

fun fact

ROSÉ HUES

Working in retail, I have noticed that the darker the rosé, the more often it is passed over by the customer; it's assumed that a darker color means more sweetness, but this is not true. The thickness of a grape's skin varies for different grape varietals and has nothing to do with the amount of sugar in the fruit. Even a short maceration time on a thick-skinned grape can yield a lot of color into the resulting wine. Try tasting a few rosés to understand how the varietal (and of course the terroir) influences the flavor, rather than the hue.

Italian Rosé

Aged Goat Cheese

Goat Gouda

Goat Cheddar

Garrotxa

As goat cheese ages, it tends to develop more complex flavors of fruit and salt. Sangiovese rosé is perfect with this style of cheese.

Pâté de Campagne and Negroamaro Rosé

Negroamaro is a grape grown in Puglia. The profile is smoky and earthy with notes of juniper and dried fruit. It is great with a chunky pâté packed with liver, as the rich meat works well with the jammy profile of the wine.

Flavors to Look For

- Mineral notes
- Earthy notes
- Red fruit
- Black fruit
- Acidity

Flavors to Avoid

- Cloying sweetness

Italian rosé is a large topic, but I think it's important to mention Italy as a country rich in many styles of rosé. Depending on terroir, particularly geology and climate, Italian rosé can be mineral driven, more earthy, or more fruity and can vary greatly in hue. Rosés from Sicily, where the soil is mostly comprised of volcanic rock, tend to take on mineral tones much like the wines of Provence. Rosés of Sangiovese from Piedmont are red-fruited, bright, and oftentimes more fruity. Southern Italian rosé can be darker hued and earthy with notes of smoke and cooked fruit. Abruzzo is known for Cerasuolo rosé, which is bright red and more akin to a light red wine. Italian rosés are so varied that they can be enjoyed with many types of food.

Olive Tapenade

Salty and deliciously briny, this spread is a perfect add to your next cheese and wine board.

MAKES ¼ CUP [65 G]

½ cup [70 g] pitted olives (green, black, kalamata, or an equal mix of all three)
1 Tbsp capers
2 garlic cloves
2 Tbsp extra-virgin olive oil
1 tsp fresh lemon juice

Place all the ingredients in a blender or food processor and process until the mixture resembles a rough paste. The tapenade can be refrigerated in an airtight container for up to 5 days.

Pizza and Cerasuolo Rosé

Cerasuolo rosé is typically made with Montepulciano d'Abruzzo grapes, which are named after the east-central region of Italy (Abruzzo) and town (Montepulciano) they come from. These rosés are slightly more vinous and can take on the bold flavors of pizza's acidic tomato sauce and fatty cheese.

Fish Stew and Sicilian Rosé

A robust fish stew with a lot of shellfish is heaven with a mineral-laden, volcanic rosé from Sicily. The shellfish create a sauce with their briny liquid that will complement the already savory rosé.

fun fact

BLENDS

Rosé can be made by a winemaker simply blending red and white wines together. It may seem like cheating, but the results can sometimes be quite good. (Don't try it at home—results may vary and probably won't be as tasty.)

Pinot Noir

Semi-Firm Sheep's and Cow's Milk Cheese

Ossau-Iraty

Tomme de Savoie

When you hear the word *Burgundy*, you should be thinking Pinot Noir. The most famous wines in the world are from there, mostly from a region called the Côte d'Or. You don't have to buy the fancy *cru* (i.e., vineyards of designated quality) Burgundy to taste the brilliant terroir of this region. Get a Bourgogne Rouge, or an unclassified vineyard blend, and pair it with a semi-firm cheese that's complex in flavor.

Roast Chicken

The Sonoma Coast of California, particularly the western part, is a wonderful grape-growing region because of its varying temperature index. Wines from this area are lean but generous, with rich and velvety red fruit, lovely minerality, and medium acid. I love them alongside a protein like chicken roasted with mushrooms and herbs.

Flavors to Look For

- Red fruit (raspberries, strawberries)
- Blue fruit (blueberries)
- Forest floor (wet mulch)
- Mineral earth
- Floral notes (roses, violets)
- Dried herbs
- Acidity

Flavors to Avoid

- Cooked fruit
- Muddied fruit

Pinot Noir is one of the most ubiquitous varietals enjoyed and purchased today. It is a grape that changes greatly from terroir to terroir and can be described as both light- and medium-bodied, depending on where it is grown. Pinot from a hotter climate can evoke more fruit-driven flavor profiles that many describe as being sweet. This sweetness isn't due to residual sugar in the wine itself, but is the result of more concentrated fruit sugars in the grapes that came about through more developed ripening. Because of its thinner skin, Pinot tends to be a less tannic wine, which makes it better to pair with a broader variety of dishes. This section will give you a broad understanding of what to expect from different styles of this varietal.

The Perfect Roast Chicken

SERVES 4

One 5 to 6 lb [2.3 to 2.7 kg] roasting chicken, rinsed and patted dry

Kosher salt

Freshly ground black pepper

1 large bunch fresh thyme

1 lemon, halved

1 head garlic, halved crosswise

2 Tbsp butter, melted

1 yellow onion, thickly sliced

Preheat the oven to 425°F [220°C]. Place the chicken in a large roasting pan and liberally season the inside of the chicken with salt and pepper. Stuff the cavity with the thyme, lemon halves, and garlic halves. Brush the outside of the chicken with the butter and sprinkle with more salt and pepper. Tie the legs of the chicken together with kitchen string and tuck the wing tips under the body of the chicken. Scatter the onion slices around the chicken in the pan. Roast for 1½ hours, or until the juices run clear when you cut between a leg and thigh. To serve the chicken, use a sharp knife to cut right through the breastbone, breaking the chicken in two halves. Then you can easily separate the breast from the leg portion, making four pieces for bigger eaters or cutting each breast in half to make six pieces in total. For storage, separate the meat from the bone and save the carcass in the freezer for making stock another day.

Truffles

Oregon is an amazing place, as it not only produces unique, terroir-driven Pinot Noir, but it also is the only state that produces edible and delicious indigenous truffles. Oregon truffles thrive in the rich and fertile land around vineyards, and many of the wines, like those in the Willamette Valley, pick up the concentrated umami in this fungus-laden earth. More blue-fruited, these wines go fantastically with rich meats and starches that are perfumed with truffles.

Sausage

Bratwurst

Lamb merguez

German Spätburgunder, a Pinot Noir made in Germany, tends to be more medium bodied, with notes of forest floor and umami. It is similarly great with mushrooms and truffles, but I really like it with game meats, especially when they are in tubular form, which pair well with the wine's earthy, meaty quality.

fun fact

CLIMATE CHANGE
AND PICKING

As we continue to see the results of climate change, winemakers are pressured to harvest their grapes earlier due to faster ripening times. Thin-skinned grapes like Pinot Noir are more susceptible to warmer temperatures; acid levels will decrease, fruit notes change from red to blue to more jammy, and nuances in minerality vary greatly.

Gamay

Fresh Goat Cheese or Chèvre

Beaujolais-Villages is made from a blend of vineyards in Beaujolais, and because of that, it is usually more eco-nomical (think Bourgogne Rouge). Like all Gamay from Beaujolais, it is very red-fruited in character, particularly expressing sour cherry and raspberry. I am not usually one to pair fresh cheeses and red wines, but the combi-nation of Gamay and fresh chèvre cre-ate a cherry cheesecake in your mouth that is undeniably delicious.

Speck

Juliénas, a cru of Beaujolais, is more serious and brooding, thanks to a var-ied soil composition of granite, alluvial river soil, and clay. It has darker notes of forest floor and mineral earth, as well as notes of wet leaves and cur-rant. I love Juliénas with cured meat, especially speck. The smoked and cured meat works with the earth-driven aspects of this Gamay.

Flavors to Look For

- Red fruit
- Black fruit
- Black tea
- Clove
- Violet

Flavors to Avoid

- Stemmy notes
- High acidity
- Jammy fruit

Gamay is a grape that many people know as Beaujolais. Beaujolais is the region the grape is indigenous to and where it's most well known— especially for the *Nouveau* (i.e., un-aged) version of it that we see during Thanksgiving time. Gamay has the body of Pinot Noir but tends to be higher in acid, fruitier, and more floral. Like all wines, Gamay is very different depending on where it is grown. Domestically, we mostly see it from California and Oregon. French Gamay mostly grows in Beaujolais, Burgundy, the Loire Valley, and the Rhône Valley. Try it as an alternative to Pinot Noir.

Basic Fruit Compote

Keep this no-fuss compote at the ready—paired with a healthy spread of goat cheese on a baguette—for impromptu snack breaks.

MAKES 1 CUP [300 G]

½ cup [100 g] granulated sugar
¾ cup [approximately 100 g] fresh or frozen fruit (such as blueberries, strawberries, or cranberries)
1 tsp grated citrus zest (such as orange, lemon, or lime)

In a small saucepan over medium heat, combine the sugar, fruit, citrus zest, and 2 Tbsp of water and bring to a boil. Turn the heat to low and simmer, stirring occasionally, until the compote has thickened and the fruit is soft and has burst, 10 to 15 minutes.

Set aside to cool (the compote will thicken as it cools). The compote can be refrigerated in an airtight container for up to 1 week.

Duck

Duck liver mousse
Seared duck breast
Duck confit

Oregon Gamay, or Gamay Noir as it sometimes is referred to, expresses blue fruit like blueberries and plums. The wine is more medium bodied and tends to display a dustier minerality with violet floral tones, which pairs amazingly with duck in its many forms.

Pork Loin

Another cru of Beaujolais, Fleurie is the most delicate. Most of Fleurie is planted on pink granite, which tends to make the wine more generous in fruit. It is lithe with definitive rose petal, clove, and lingonberry. It has a more linear profile with a high-toned elegance that balances its supple texture. It is wonderful with fatty meats like pork. I love it paired with a seared loin and served with a red-fruit compote on the side.

fun fact

CARBONIC FERMENTATION

Most Gamay is fermented carbonically to produce a more accessible, fruit-driven wine. Grapes are added to the press with their vines and leaves intact, a process known as *whole cluster*. Because of an excess of other matter, a canopy is created in a tank or barrel that prevents oxygen from thriving and builds up carbon dioxide gas. These gases develop within the berry skin, creating many tiny fermenting capsules that will then begin to burst. This reaction changes the texture of the resulting wine and creates a fun effervescence.

Frappato

Herbed Goat Cheese

I am usually not a proponent of flavored cheese, but I do love fresh cheeses that are enhanced by local herbs and botanicals. Goat cheese that is coated in herbes de Provence or another savory and aromatic combination is able to complement the flavors and texture of a light red like Frappato. The subtle smoke and minerality of the wine complement the herbaceous brightness of the cheese.

Country Pâté

Frappato and most charcuterie will be a successful pairing, but I especially love this wine paired with the rustic, chunky texture of pâté de campagne. This dish often combines flavorings like clove, allspice, and sometimes juniper berry, which complement the warm earthiness of the volcanic wine.

Flavors to Look For

- Raspberry
- Quince
- Rose

Flavors to Avoid

- Vegetal
- Jammy fruit
- High acidity
- Overly floral

Frappato is a grape that you may not have heard of but should definitely get to know. It is indigenous to Sicily and is representative of lighter reds that prosper in volcanic-rich soil. It is grown in the southeastern part of the island, mostly in the area called Vittoria where there is a predominance of limestone rock, clay, iron, and other volcanic rock matter. The soil composition is unique in that it prevented phylloxera (a pernicious pest that killed much of the vines in western Europe in the mid-1800s) from taking hold in Sicily, which accounts for the abundance of very old vines. Famously, it is blended with another varietal called Nero d'Avola to produce the blend called Cerasuolo di Vittoria. Frappato is light- to medium-bodied with assertive notes of rose petal, high-toned minerality, and smoke. It is great chilled and young or is lovely aged. It pairs well with many types of food, from antipasti to rich seafood stews.

Herby Goat Cheese

Goat cheese, with its fresh, subtle notes, is the perfect vessel for a bevy of flavors. For a sweet twist, substitute a healthy dollop of fruit compote for the herbes de Provence and pollen.

SERVES 4

2 tsp herbes de Provence
1 tsp fennel pollen
One 8 oz [230 g] log fresh goat cheese
1 Tbsp extra-virgin olive oil
Toasted bread, for serving

Mix together the herbs and fennel pollen until distributed and spread the mixture on a cutting board. Gently roll the goat cheese in the mixture, coating all sides. Place the log on a cheese board or platter and drizzle with the olive oil. Serve the cheese with toasted bread.

Bouillabaisse

Frappato is wonderful paired with fish stews like bouillabaisse. The enriched shellfish broth is a nice complement to the briny notes in the wine. Spices like saffron and herbs like thyme go with it nicely, as does the hit of Pernod, a licorice-scented liqueur that is oftentimes included in the recipe.

Lamb

Lamb is an ingredient that is sometimes overpowering for some light reds, but Frappato has the mineral backbone to take on the gamey meat. I would try it with lamb loin or chops, simply grilled and flavored with salt, pepper, and fresh lemon juice. The char on the meat complements the smoke that is inherent in the volcanic wine, and the wine's supple texture and red-fruit quality balance out the gaminess in the lamb.

fun fact

AMPHORA REDS

Frappato is sometimes aged in amphora, which is a clay vessel that dates back to the Neolithic period. The material allows the oxygenation of the wine without the addition of any oak flavors. The practice of aging wine in amphorae is common in Greece and on islands like Sicily and is also an ancient practice of aging skin-contact wines in Georgia.

Zinfandel

Blue Cheese

Roquefort
Stilton

Aged Zin carries a weight and rich fruit quality that can stand in for port wine. I love to pair this style of Zinfandel with blue cheeses. Roquefort is a bright and piquant sheep's milk blue that enhances the flavor of the fruit-laden wine, while the barnyardy notes of Stilton create an earthy pairing that is satisfyingly savory.

'Nduja

'Nduja is a spreadable pork-based salume that is flavored with roasted peppers and spices. It can be added to a sauce, used as a condiment, or simply spread on baguette. The chewy texture of Zinfandel and its black fruit temper the heat of the 'nduja while accentuating the herbs and spices.

Flavors to Look For

- Blackberry jam
- Bramble
- Dried fruit
- Licorice
- Acidity

Flavors to Avoid

- Candied fruit
- Muddied fruit

Zinfandel is a full-bodied red wine that is driven by rich fruit and a mouth-coating texture. Indigenous to Croatia, it is also quite common in California and southern Italy, where it is known as Primitivo. Zin is a grape that can thrive in hotter temperatures, and its thick skin tends to extract more color and tannin into the wine. A highly structured red, Zin has a lovely balance of ripe to cooked black fruit (blackberries, huckleberries), holiday spice (allspice and clove), and forest floor (mulch and wet leaves). The best Zins are complex and have bright and herbaceous elements that lift it from tasting like stewed fruit. The boldness of Zinfandel makes it a trickier wine to pair, but its robust flavor creates a suitable complement to other strong-flavored foods.

Easy 'Nduja

This Italian spread is a flavorful way to add in a bit of spice. Try serving with roasted vegetables, dotting on your favorite pizza, or spreading on crusty bread.

1 cup [125 g] finely diced soppressata

3 Tbsp extra-virgin olive oil

2 Tbsp minced Calabrian chiles

2 Tbsp minced sun-dried tomatoes

Combine all of the ingredients in a food processor or blender and pulse until smooth, or to your desired consistency. Use as a spread in sandwiches for a deep, spicy hit of flavor. Store in an air-tight container in the refrigerator for up to 2 weeks.

Barbecued Ribs and Hamburgers

Zinfandel is wonderful with anything grilled; there is something about the flavor of the char mixed with the rich fruit that works so well. It is a great wine to have alongside pork ribs slathered with barbecue sauce or a hamburger topped with bacon and blue cheese.

Pizza

Zinfandel is the definitive pizza wine. The acid of the tomato sauce and cheese pair supremely with this mouth-coating red. It is great with a meat-laden pie or a simple Margherita.

fun fact

BOOZY ZIN

Many Zinfandels have a higher alcohol-to-volume ratio than other wines. This is primarily due to the fact that these thick-skinned grapes can withstand hot temperatures without breaking down. They are grown in places with longer growing seasons and can hang out longer, ripening to their fullest extent. The tannins and fruit presence of a Zin tend to keep the wine balanced, making it seem less alcoholic than it is.

Bordeaux

Pairing 1

Washed-Rind Cheese

Époisses
Taleggio

This is a very savory pairing. Washed-rind cheeses like Époisses and Taleggio have a lot of cured- and smoked-meat notes that are similarly present in the wine. Texturally, creamier cheeses are going to pair better with bigger, more tannic wines like Bordeaux (whereas cheeses with less moisture can be too dry on the palate).

Pairing 2

Blood Sausage

Iron-rich meats are particularly delicious with Bordeaux from the Left Bank that are mostly comprised of Cabernet Sauvignon. The wine and the sausage both have a pronounced minerality that is very complementary. Cabernet tends to express notes of mint and tarragon, which is quite pleasant with the strong-flavored, offal-based sausage.

Flavors to Look For

- Leather
- Tobacco
- Mint
- Black cherry
- Beef
- Black tea

Flavors to Avoid

- Harsh tannins without balance of fruit
- Tar
- Bandage (Brettanomyces, see Bordeaux)

Bordeaux is a red blend that takes its name from the city in the south-west of France. Bordeaux blends range in varietal depending on where they are made: Left Bank Bordeaux is Cabernet Sauvignon dominant, while the Right Bank favors Merlot. The Médoc region sees a more generous inclusion of Cabernet Franc, Petit Verdot, and Malbec. Depending on the composition, the wine can be on the tannic side with more earthy, leathery notes, or more fruit-driven with notes of cooked fruit and Christmas spices. These are full-bodied reds that are structured for aging, which can make it a challenge to successfully pair foods with them. Through trial and error, I have learned that Cabernet-dominant Bordeaux are slightly more forgiving when aged longer to smooth their tannins, while young wines from the Merlot-dominant Right Bank can be more approachable.

Charcuterie Board

I love a good charcuterie board. It makes for the perfect lunch or dinner and is great for sharing. A Merlot-based Right Bank Bordeaux is the perfect accompaniment to cold meats, pickles, and spreads. Pork fat and red wine is truly a match made in Bordeaux.

SERVES 4 TO 6

8 oz [230 g] slice country pâté (I love the ones studded with dried fruit like currants or figs and nuts like pistachio)

8 oz [230 g] or 6 to 8 slices speck (you could substitute prosciutto)

8 oz [230 g] or 6 to 8 slices bresaola (you could use beef, pork, or game)

6 oz [170 g] smooth duck liver mousse (served in the jar or in a quenelle shape on the board)

6 oz [170 g] cornichons

4 oz [115 g] whole-grain mustard

1 baguette, sliced into rounds

Arrange the various meats on a big board with the cornichons, mustard, and bread rounds. Pour out some glasses of wine and enjoy.

Prime Rib

During the holiday season, you will always see my table decked with prime rib and an aged Right Bank Bordeaux. Prime rib, cooked medium rare, is a delicate meat and I like the way it pairs with the fruit presence in the Merlot-dominant Bordeaux. Age smooths out the tannins and acidity, enhancing the velvety texture of this wine as it envelops the tender beef.

Coq au Vin

Bordeaux can be tough to pair with lighter meat dishes, but coq au vin is anything but that. Layered with a rich wine-based sauce and laden with earthy mushrooms and herbs, this chicken dish is a perfect match for a big, full-bodied wine like Bordeaux. I love it when the wine has a nice percentage of Cabernet Franc, to give it a more peppery bite.

fun fact

YEAST

Brettanomyces is a type of yeast that produces sensory compounds when it is present in wine. Although the flavor is enjoyed by beer brewers, it is not a welcome guest in the winery; flavors like bandage, barnyard, cheese, and just over-all rancidity can result when this yeast is present in wines (I've noticed it in Bordeaux and certain Syrah). Vintners need to be extra careful since it can live and thrive in the winery atmosphere.

Syrah

Salty Sheep's Milk Cheese

Pyrénées sheep's milk cheese
Manchego

I like to pair semi-firm sheep's milk cheeses with Syrah from Cornas in the northern Rhône or from the western United States. The wines from these areas express blueberry or huckleberry fruit that work beautifully with the salty, gamey notes in the cheese.

Duck Confit

Whether more earth driven or fruit forward, Syrah goes superbly with duck confit. The natural fatty notes in the wine pair well with the flavors of the rendered fat in the duck. Serve with a reduced sauce of blueberry or currant to bring this pairing to the next level.

Flavors to Look For

- Graphite
- Blue fruit (blueberries)
- Leather
- Baking spices
- Animal fat

Flavors to Avoid

- Bandage (Brettanomyces, see Bordeaux)
- Acetone (volatile acidity)

Syrah can range from medium- to full-bodied depending on where and how it is made. Syrah is most famously grown in the Rhône River Valley in France. North of the river, it shines prominently in the wines from Côte Rôtie, Cornas, Crozes-Hermitage, and Saint-Joseph. In the south, it is blended with Grenache to perfect wines from Gigondas, Vacqueyras, and the Côtes du Rhône. Syrah is also grown in the United States, specifically in the West (Washington, Oregon, and California), and tends to be less brooding than its French counterpart. In the Southern Hemisphere, it takes on the name *Shiraz* in Australia and is also growing well in Argentina and other parts of South America. Syrah has wonderful pairing potential because it tends to be well-balanced in fruit and earth elements and has medium tannins that enhance rather than overpower.

Yakitori-Style Grilled Mushrooms

Try pairing this weeknight meal with a smooth, lower-tannin Syrah, which will cut through the umami notes of the grilled mushrooms.

SERVES 2

⅓ cup [80 ml] mirin

⅓ cup [80 ml] sake

⅓ cup [80 ml] soy sauce

⅓ cup [65 g] raw sugar

12 oz [340 g] large mushrooms (such as shiitake, portobello, or king trumpet), trimmed, halved lengthwise, and cut crosswise into 2 in [5 cm] pieces

1 tsp vegetable oil

Kosher salt

1 green onion, thinly sliced

In a small saucepan over medium heat, bring the mirin, sake, soy sauce, and sugar to a boil. Turn down the heat to low and simmer until slightly reduced, 12 to 15 minutes; set aside. Thread pieces onto a skewer (aim for three pieces per skewer), brush the mushrooms lightly with the oil, and season lightly with salt. Heat a grill pan over medium-high heat, add the mushrooms, and grill until golden brown, about 1 minute per side. Brush the mushrooms with the sauce and continue to grill, turning occasionally, until glazed and tender, about 2 minutes. Top with the green onion and serve immediately.

Roasted or Braised Lamb

Syrah and game meats are particularly well suited. Lamb braised in a rich red wine sauce or roasted with herbs is complemented by a Syrah from the northern Rhône. Either a Cornas or Côte Rôtie will bring blue fruit and bramble notes, which is perfect with the meat.

Mushrooms

Whether you are including mushrooms in a meat-focused dish or going entirely vegetarian, Syrah is a good option for a full-bodied accompaniment. Syrah from Washington tends to express notes of forest floor and is not usually as big and tannic as the wines from the northern Rhône, making it a good option for a mushroom-laden main.

fun fact

GOOD BACTERIA

Volatile acidity is an aromatic element of wine, which is mostly caused by bacteria. The ascetic acid that is created from it is gaseous and gives off an aroma like vinegar or acetone. Bacteria can thrive better in old barrels because they tend to be less sterile. It is very common, but some wines have more than others, and too much can be overpowering.

•

Dessert Wines

Aged Dutch Gouda and Madeira

Aged cow's milk Gouda is intensely salty with notes of caramel, roasted nuts, and dried apricot. It is tremendous paired with a madeira that is similarly sweet and nutty. Together, the pairing brings forth an umami flavor like sweet braised meat or mushrooms.

Blue Cheese and Ruby Port

Blue cheese, especially the grassier versions like Gorgonzola, pair wonderfully with a ruby port that is sweet yet bursting with fresh blue-fruit notes. The port tempers the almost briny salt of the cheese and creates a berry-cheesecake flavor.

Flavors to Look For

- Dried fruit
- Tree nuts
- Citrus
- White flowers
- Baking spices

Flavors to Avoid

- Muddied fruit
- Cloying sweetness
- High-proof alcohol

Dessert wines can be made from picking late harvest, botrytized, or frozen grapes. Whether it's from the sun, a fungal interaction, or freezing temperatures, the common thread in all these cases is that the sugars in the grape juice become concentrated, making the wines sweeter. When fermenting these wines, the winemaker chooses to stop the process before all the sugar is transformed into alcohol. This allows the wine to retain a certain level of sweetness, and it keeps the alcohol levels low as well.

Fortified wines are wines that are kept sweet by the addition of a higher-proof alcohol stopping fermentation before all the sugar is used. Common fortified wines are port, sherry, and madeira, and depending on the maker and the recipe, these can vary in sweetness.

As we discussed with sweet Riesling, some of the most interesting food pairings with sweet wines are not sweet themselves. Moreover, sweet wines and fortified wines can take on even stronger, more robust flavors due to their intensity and denser body.

Hot Buttered Port

Dark and sweet, this drink is ideal for warming up and getting cozy.

SERVES 2

1½ cups [360 ml] port
4 tsp light honey
2 tsp butter

In a medium saucepan, heat the port and 5 oz [150 ml] of water over high heat until just simmering. Add 2 tsp of the honey and 1 tsp of the butter into each heat-safe glass. Pour the heated wine mixture into the glasses and stir to mix the butter and honey before serving.

Sweet Nightcap

This easy-to-make cocktail is the perfect way to unwind at the end of the day.

SERVES 1

1½ oz [45 ml] sweet vermouth
2 oz [60 ml] sparkling water
3 dashes Angostura bitters
Orange curl, for garnish

Add the vermouth, sparkling water, and bitters to a highball glass filled with ice. Gently stir to combine, garnish with an orange curl, and serve.

Sauternes and Summer Sausage

Sauternes, a dessert wine from Bordeaux, is usually served just with dessert, but I like it with the spice and salt of a summer sausage. Make sure the wine is suitably chilled, otherwise it can be too cloying.

Late Harvest Riesling and Cheesecake

The floral notes and high acid of a late harvest Riesling pair incredibly well with the lactic acidity and sweetness of cheesecake, as the dessert's delicious fattiness is balanced out by the wine. Serve the cake with seasonal fresh fruit and whipped cream for extra decadence.

fun fact

SIPPING SWEETLY

Sweet vermouths are a great alternative to an after-dinner dessert wine. They are infused with fragrant roots and herbs and then sugared to balance the bitterness. They are slightly fortified, so their alcohol by volume is 15 to 17 percent, lower than other fortified wines, like ports, which sit at around 20 percent. The lower alcohol content in vermouths allows them to be sold at stores without a liquor license. Cutting a sweet vermouth with sparkling water will create an easy nightcap that can act as a digestif.

Party
Planning

When you're trying to plan a party, the easiest way to begin might be to think of a vision or scope for the event. If you are planning to pair wines with different cheeses, meats, or dishes, is there a way to connect the dots thematically through geography, food styles, ingredients, or flavors? Another key question to ask yourself is, *What is the star of the show?* If food is the primary focus, the wines can just be there to complement and support the flavors of the foods. A hot-and-spicy Thai-themed meal could be supported with wines that are bright, have high acidity, and include some residual sugar, but there is no pressure to find wines made in Thailand or Southeast Asia.

That being said, I love planning meals around regional dishes and wines from my travels. Once you understand the focus of your menu, you can use the tenets in this book to support you in the pairing process. The phrase "what grows together goes together" is a philosophy that surely inspired the world's very first pairing parties, and it continues to prove effective. In many cases, it is easy to find these specialized components. However, it may take some research to uncover less common indigenous ingredients, so don't be afraid to ask your local wine specialists and food retailers to help in your hunt for certain items.

Cheese

Every wine section in this book has one or two cheese pairings to give credence to the great partnership the two share. Essentially, cheese is fatty, and wine is acidic. This combination is inherently cleansing to the palate because most of the fat is washed away by the wine, creating once again a neutral zone that is ready to welcome more flavor. In order to give the care and consideration that wine's best friend deserves, here are some tips and tricks to take your cheese pairing to a whole new level.

CHEESE STYLES

This is a basic list of cheese styles to keep in mind. This list is in order from mildest to strongest.

FRESH: These are very young cheeses that do not present any rind development. For the purposes of pairing, fresh cheese is the mildest and most nuanced in flavor, thus making it easily overpowered.

SURFACE-RIPENED: Like Brie, Camembert, and triple-creams, these are cheeses that have developed a thin rind to encase their paste. The category "surface-ripened" refers to the way they ripen from the outside in. Slightly more aged than fresh, they have developed more complexity of flavor, often possessing more vegetal notes like brassicas and mushrooms.

SEMI-FIRM: Semi-firm cheeses are those that still have some give when touched but contain less moisture than the two previous categories. Cheeses like Manchego, young Gouda, and younger Alpine cheese might be classified as semi-firm.

FIRM: Firm cheeses are sometimes aged for over a year and have lost most, if not all, of their moisture content. This length of cellaring introduces strong flavors to these cheeses, including salted caramel, nuts, beef bouillon, and dried mushroom. Parmigiano-Reggiano, aged Dutch Gouda, English Cheddar, and Gruyère would be included here.

SMEAR-RIPENED/WASHED-RIND: These cheeses have a wash—which can vary from a brine to an alcohol, such as beer, wine, or brandy—that is applied during the aging process. This encourages the growth of bacteria that interact with oxygen to produce pungent aromas and tastes. Examples of washed-rind cheeses are Époisses, Taleggio, and Fontina.

BLUE: Blue cheeses get their strong flavor from both the piquant mold they feature as well as the cultures included in their recipe. Blue cheese can be made with any type of milk, which also creates variance in flavor.

A rind is more or less a jacket that a cheese grows for protection during its life. Rinds can add a lot of flavor to the paste of cheese when eaten together. They help you understand the terroir or place a cheese came from before it came to be on the retail shelf. Natural rinds are found on surface-ripened cheeses like Brie, washed-rind cheeses, semi-firms, and firms. They develop from the mix of molds and yeasts in the atmosphere of cheese caves. The younger the cheese, the younger the rind and the milder it will taste. All-natural rinds are edible, but as cheese ages, their rinds do become thicker and mustier. Keep in mind that they will influence a pairing, and it may not be for the better. It goes without saying that rinds can also be made of other less appetizing materials; wax, paper, and muslin cloth are applied by the cheese maker to foster longevity while aging. Rinds can add a lot of aesthetic beauty and texture to a cheese board, and while some guests may choose to cut them off, others may want to experience their taste.

CUTTING (WHICH SHAPES FOR WHICH CHEESES)

When cutting cheeses for a platter, it is important to take into account the ratio of rind to paste so that every guest gets a fair portion. Here are some tips for how to cut and serve cheeses by their categories.

- I like to serve fresh cheese in a dumpling-like oval shape, also known as a *quenelle*, using two spoons for shaping. Surface-ripened cheese can be cut like pieces of a cake, where the paste is encased by the rind on the top and bottom.

- For the most part, semi-firm cheeses can be cut into wedges, as they retain enough moisture and elasticity to maintain their shape.

- Firm cheeses that are drier must be chunked into pieces. Discard any waxed or very thick rinds, which are caused by continuous aging, making them inedible.

- Serving washed-rind cheeses depends on the level of ripeness. Runny ones can be spooned directly on the plate, while less ripe ones can be cut like other surface-ripened cheese.

- Blues without rinds tend to have a crumbly texture and benefit from chunking, but some with natural rinds can successfully be wedged.

HOW TO SET UP A CHEESE PLATE

When setting up a cheese plate, especially for the purposes of pairing, it is essential to organize the cheeses from the mildest to the most robust in flavor. This can be arranged on a rectangular platter horizontally or on a round surface in a clockwise order. As you pair different wines with the cheeses, you will continue to build flavor complexity, so you do not want your palate to become fatigued in the process. The flavor of a style of cheese is intentional (most of the time), and time, as well as added process decisions (like washing or wrapping of the rind), can augment a cheese's flavor.

In most cases, the younger the cheese, the milder it will be. Fresh cheeses like chèvre, fresh sheep's milk cheese, cow's milk fromage blanc, ricotta, or burrata should be tasted and paired before stronger-flavored cheeses like washed-rind, blue, Cheddar, and Gouda. Even more nuanced, milk types impart different flavors, so the order of cheeses within categories (e.g., fresh, semi-firm, etc.) might be important depending on how precise you want your tasting to be. Remember, cheese is a living product that changes slightly each time you encounter it, so it's important to taste ahead of your guests' arrival to confirm the order of things.

WRAPPING (HOW BEST TO KEEP CHEESE)

When a cheese is cut from its whole form and then rewrapped, the length of time it will stay fresh (and delicious) is shortened drastically. If you don't have the right equipment, each time you cut off pieces of a cheese and rewrap the leftovers, this process compounds itself. If you can, it is best to use paper made specifically for cheese that has a wax coating on the outside and a porous plastic on the inside. This paper promotes an exchange of oxygen while limiting the moisture that can be released.

Young cheese and fresh cheese that contain a lot of moisture should be eaten more quickly than those that are more aged and drier. Off-flavors resulting from unwelcome bacteria and molds will proliferate in these moisture-laden cheeses. When wrapped and stored correctly, aged cheeses will still develop molds over time, but these can usually be simply cut off the surface of the cheese.

Meat

Charcuterie is an easy accompaniment to wine. When deciding which cuts and cures to choose, the main things to keep in mind are salt and fat. Both salt and fat make charcuterie satisfying and delicious, but too much of either can make a pairing unbalanced. Here are some suggestions to remember when trying to pair wine and meat:

DRY BUBBLES AND FAT

- Prosciutto

- Lardo

- Guanciale

SWEET OR FRUITY BUBBLES WITH SALT AND GAME MEATS

- Pork salami

- Boar sausage

DRY WHITES WITH FORCEMEAT

- Mortadella

SWEET WHITES

- Spicy salami
- 'Nduja
- Liver

ROSÉ

- Confit duck
- Rillettes
- Lamb sausage

LIGHT REDS

- Game meats, like duck prosciutto
- Liver
- Country pâté

DARK REDS

These are more difficult to pair with charcuterie unless they are more jammy and fruit-driven. Zinfandel and Petite Syrah are good options and work well with salty and gamey meat.

Fruit, Nuts, and All the Rest

For when you want to offer something beyond the standard meat-and-cheese platter, here are some suggested pairings to create a quick party spread built around other accoutrements:

FRESH FRUIT

- Fresh cheese
- Sparkling, dry, and sweet whites
- Fattier charcuterie

DRIED FRUIT

- Semi-firm cheese
- Light reds
- Salty, hard salami

COMPOTE/JAM/HONEY

- Washed-rind and blue cheeses
- Sweet wine and sparkling wine
- Meat pâté, mousse, and fat-preserved meat

- Semi-firm cheese

- Fuller whites

- Salty meats, like hard salami

Bread and crackers are solid and versatile vessels for layering cheeses, meats, and other nibbles, so deciding between them should depend on your and your company's tastes. You could choose from:

- Roughly cut baguette slices

- Sea salt crackers

- Whole-wheat crisps

- Sesame crackers

- Pita slices

- Crostini

- Butter crackers

- Pepper water crackers

- Lavash

Resources

This list is by no means exhaustive, so I encourage you to seek out your local wine shops to discover what they have in store for you.

WEST COAST

Bay Area, CA

Arlequin Wine Merchant
www.arlequinwinemerchant.com

Bay Grape
www.baygrapewine.com

Bi-Rite Market
www.biritemarket.com

Gemini Bottle Co.
www.geminibottlesf.com

Ordinaire
www.ordinairewine.com

Palm City Wines
www.palmcitysf.com

Ruby Wine
www.rubywinesf.com

Los Angeles, CA

Corner Shop
www.cornershopla.com

Domaine LA
www.domainela.com

Lou Wine Shop
www.louwineshop.com

Psychic Wines
www.psychicwinesla.com

Portland, OR

Ardor Natural Wines
www.ardornaturalwines.com

Bar Norman
www.barnorman.com

SOUTH

Tucson, AZ

Westbound
www.westboundtucson.com

New Orleans, LA

Bacchanal Wines
www.bacchanalwine.com

Faubourg Wines
www.faubourgwines.com

Austin, TX

LoLo Wines
www.lolo.wine

Houston, TX

Light Years Wine
www.lightyearswine.com

Charleston, SC

Monarch Wine Merchants
www.monarchwinemerchants.com

MIDWEST

Chicago, IL

Diversey Wine
www.diverseywine.com

Foxtrot
www.foxtrotco.com

Red & White Wines
*www.red-white-wines-chicago
.myshopify.com*

EAST COAST

Baltimore, MD

Angels Ate Lemons
www.angelsatelemons.com

Fadensønnen
www.fadensonnen.com

District of Columbia

Domestique
www.domestiquewine.com

New York, NY

Chambers Street Wines
www.chambersstwines.com

Frankly Wines
www.franklywines.com

Henry's Wine & Spirit
www.henrys.nyc

Peoples Wine
www.peoples.wine

Vine Wine
www.vine-wine.com

CHEESE SHOPS

WEST COAST

Bay Area, CA

Bi-Rite Market
www.biritemarket.com

The Cheese Board Collective
www.cheeseboardcollective.coop

Market Hall
www.rockridgemarkethall.com

Los Angeles, CA

DTLA Cheese
www.dtlacheese.com

Say Cheese
www.saycheeselosangeles.com

EAST COAST

Boston, MA

Formaggio Kitchen
www.formaggiokitchen.com

New York, NY

Bedford Cheese Shop
www.bedfordcheeseshop.com

Murray's
www.murrayscheese.com

SOUTH

Sarasota, FL

Artisan Cheese Company
www.artisancheesecompany.com

Austin, TX

Antonelli's Cheese Shop
www.antonellischeese.com

MIDWEST

Ann Arbor, MI

Zingerman's Creamery
www.zingermanscreamery.com

St. Paul, MN

St. Paul Cheese Shop
www.stpaulcheeseshop.com

Acknowledgments

I am very thankful to everyone who contributed to making this book possible. Thank you to Chronicle Books for supporting me in this venture. My editor, Dena Rayess, has been a tremendous anxiety reducer. Thank you to my girlfriend, Emily, for always understanding, and to my friends and colleagues in the wine industry in San Francisco for always being a constant source of inspiration and love.

Library of Congress Cataloging-in-Publication Data.

Names: Rubin, Liz, author.
Title: Wine pairing party : 16 wine profiles. 80 perfect food pairings. /
  by Liz Rubin.
Description: San Francisco : Chronicle Books, [2022]
Identifiers: LCCN 2021011499 | ISBN 9781797203461 (hardcover)
Subjects: LCSH: Food and wine pairing. | Cooking.
Classification: LCC TX911.3.M45 R83 2022 | DDC 641.2/2--dc23
LC record available at https://lccn.loc.gov/2021011499

Manufactured in China.

Design by **Vanessa Dina**.

10 9 8 7 6 5 4 3 2 1

Chronicle books and gifts are available at special quantity discounts to
corporations, professional associations, literacy programs, and other
organizations. For details and discount information, please contact our
premiums department at corporatesales@chroniclebooks.com or at
1-800-759-0190.

Chronicle Books LLC
680 Second Street
San Francisco, California 94107
www.chroniclebooks.com